AF242006

A MIDDLE-AGED WOMAN RAGES

A Middle-Aged Woman Rages

by

Melissa Jørgenrud Helton

Accents Publishing • Lexington, Kentucky • 2026

Copyright © 2026 by Melissa Jørgenrud Helton
All rights reserved

Printed in the United States of America

Accents Publishing
Editor: Katerina Stoykova
Cover Image: *Soap Bubble*, Alexandre-Blaise Desgoffe, 1882

Library of Congress Control Number: 2026940241
ISBN: 978-1-961127-25-8
First Edition

Accents Publishing is an independent press for brilliant voices. For a catalog of current and upcoming titles, please visit us on the Web at

www.accents-publishing.com

CONTENTS

To all the middle-aged women
who raged before me and showed the way,
and to all the middle-aged women beside me now,
with clear, brawny voices.

★

But it's never really rage, is it?

It's self-defense. It's grief.
It's the crying out of the birthed
and the birthing. It's an iceberg
flipping upside down and showing
the enormous, honest jade mass
of itself, striped with black.
It's saying everything that came
before this moment was circus
house mirrors, was involuntary
intoxication. She never really rages
the way a man rages, the way late July
rages, the way a smoke alarm rages.
Instead, it is a new hickory sucker,
spouted desperately from the cut,
bending and bending and bending
and bending and bending until
the wood fibers tear and splay.
Her not-really-rage is a pot rusting
in the rain until it stains whatever it's
sitting on. It is some night creature
slinking out to drag off the dead
cardinal the escaped housecat
so unnecessarily killed
and left on the porch.

SHE UNDERSTANDS VESUVIUS

with her heart of pyroclastic flow
and all the hidden echoes of bodies.
The storytellers will come 1,800
years later and fill the empty spaces
with plaster. They so want to see and study
and gasp at the postures of quick death.

HIDDEN NAMING

My female body is a bitch,
eternal hunger and bruise.
Leaden skies gather, swell
in between breaths. Sleet
shivers the window ginkgo,
shushes this neurotic skin
and blustery mind—

    in the end it comes down to a slap
reddening a cheek, the virus's aria
elongating the third encore's fever,
no end in sight. Speak now, speak
ever so gently. Remember how hope
echoing back to you squalls in the ear.

Should we forget our womanly places, a DJ
understands what to make these curves do.
Zygote to grave, these body shapes of vigor
and bounce are publicly debated, the going
net worth a group decision. Listen up girlie,
no one will like you like that, disavowing men
everywhere. We like you quieter, much softer.
    Body is a map marking green hills and bayou,
the tourist shops and where we put the dead.

THE GREAT BLACK SWAMP WOMAN

I am not a field of glistening corn to feed you or your hogs or your ethanol gas tank. I am done being your harvest, your stockpile, your safety net against war time rations and famine. I am done tying you to your history. I am done being your autumn haunted maze to design and charge admission for children to run and scream through. I am done being curated with chemical fertilizers that will spur toxic algae blooms in the lake, curated by plows and GMO seeds modified to tolerate higher and higher and higher concentration of poison, seeds that only produce sterile offspring. Fill these drainage ditches and let me back to my birthright – let me swamp again into deep mud, let the ground sloth and beavers crawl all over me, coyote, turtles, and waterbirds, a million types of insects, moss and slime and deep, terrifying fecundity fueled by rot, not factory sprays and pellets. Let my trees return so dense daylight erases, my buckeye, black locust, burr oak, willow, ironwood, and shellbark hickory canopies shading the blister sun into thick murk. Give me back my frogs and mosquitos, gnats and fish. Damselflies. Dragonflies. Ticks. Wasps. Grasshoppers. Indigo snake, snapping turtle, timber rattler, green anole, cottonmouth. Heron, egret, bittern, pileated woodpecker, barred owl, bald eagle, peregrine falcon. Mud 6-feet deep, so hungry it swallows horse legs and wagon wheels. It took only 30 years for man to undo eons, as they do. Let me rot back into being uninhabitable to men and alive with malaria and stink, alive to myself as *I* decide what survives and where and how it thrives, untethered to a dollar, a man's tractor, someone's dinner table, a capitalist hellscape and environmental disaster. Let me thrive in my swampy nature, stop drying me out for productivity. Give me my wild rice, skunk cabbage, bracken fern, water lily, bladderwort, my rabbits and ducks and muskrats, otters, and all those scary wolves. Give me back my cholera and no humans around to die of it. Let my historic life, dark and gooey and vibrant and gross return to me, unseen around these parts for the last 250 years.

THE MOON CALLS US ALL

to thrive in flux,
to pull the water
of the whole world
behind us as we go

without apology.

TOPEKA

In a gray Airbnb in Topeka that smells
of old cigarettes and fried food, trying not
to cry in the early morning, I put on

a Spotify mellow mix playlist, start to stretch
on the gray floor. I hear the gray rain coming down,
pull my awareness away from the giant,

screaming pain in my chest. I think of our route
westward, the Brown v. Board of Education
National Historical Park that we'll visit

once everyone wakes up and packs, what kind
of poem I might find there as a white woman.
And I look up to see the beige sign on the gray wall,

a big wood cutout circle that says *Yay! You're here.*
And I am. I am in this floor in Topeka. My love
and the children are sleeping, ready to float

along on the itinerary I will chisel for us
from the day's marble. *Yay! You're here.* I am.
All the doors in my head bursting open

and slamming shut, rapidfire. My heart like a pot
of thick oatmeal on the stove. The hidden
depths of boiled-off vapor is almost strong enough

to bubble the gelatinous surface up and splatter it
everyway, scalding anyone who happens to be near.
Yay! You're here. I am, and though

I am not good, I am better. And that is worth
a cheap celebration in gray Kansas.

FIRST 100 SENTENCES
of A Life Sentence, *a line-a-day journal for 25 years*

And so it begins. Happy birthday
from our little home. Sometimes,
the truth is in blood.

> *Life is like sea foam.*
> *Give yourself away like the sea.*

The lights flicker and we hold
still. It was a woulda-been day
of epic proportions.
    The serenity prayer is wise.

We venture out into the blinding snow.
    Today's postcard was a moose from the UP.

Billionaire superheroes aren't
relatable. Water shifts form again. Take a string,
knot it a thousand times.
    I saw dad, in a dream deli.
Black Widow is a metaphor
for fighting patriarchy. Decenter men
today and see how you feel.

    The day hardens too easily.

    If a man can feed you, he can starve you.

TikTok is banned, but not AR-15s. What an insult,
this inauguration on MLK day. A thousand knots
in a string makes fabric. I'll talk if you
have a camera in my face.

    Frost in my heart; frost on the trees.

History piles around us. The children
and the sun return. Jump ship
onto another ship with the same captain.
          Isn't one year still the honeymoon?

Happy ghost birthday, old man.

America got really scary
this week. These thoughts
are papercuts: small
and terrible. Rain at night
still brings nightmares.

One month down and 299 to go. The groundhog
says 6 more weeks. It'll take years
to unravel this knot.
          Paycheck to paycheck
          is stressful. I hope we sell
          this car today. Good-bye
          Mazda, it was a good
          279,210 miles.

          A sad sow in a pretty dress is still a sad sow.
The trains here are close and loud.

Mildred Haun is good family.
We haven't spoken face-to-face
since our divorce day.
It was the Queen song, but
We are the pancakes.

          16 years ago, they stripped my membranes.
          16 years ago, Violet Abigail took a breath.
          Happy heavenly bday brother Joel.
          That's enough rain for a while.

We survived another giant flood.
          Johnson City was a warm
refuge. Still no gas in our cold, cold,
house. Yesterday I became a KY Colonel.

          Flood mud covered in snow is new.

The mind is a warden.

This paradox should be celebrated.
I woke up dreaming of a flood
crochet pattern. I walk the debris-tangled
bridge. Happy heavenly birthday
Rich. Today is creek clean-up day.

I missed seeing governor Beshear.

I wish the kids were here.
We didn't go
to the Postcrossing meetup.

          Gotta get control of this house
          today. The desk light
          keeps flickering. So many things
                    remain undone.

                    Please help me carry this clock.

          We're living in the Great UpsideDown.
They worship a liar, and know he is one.

A door isn't there to serve itself.

Good morning from this hillside. Step,
and step, and step again. The evening sun
fills this room. I just put my child

as my emergency contact. This 13-minute
update has taken 27 minutes.

> *History without discomfort is propaganda.*
> Beware the Ides of March.

> Let's go see Ani Difranco!
> I bought a crow postcard.
> It says *I poop on fascists*.

It is hard to be understood.

Hundreds gathering
in community is power.
The coyotes and frost glitter
greet the morning. The animal,
child, captain, and guru rarely align.
I was harmed, yet *I'm* making the peace.

> Back at it, as expected.
> Stop begging.
> Negative self-talk is so uninteresting.

> I want to dance with you.

A spoon is inked into skin. The youngins
will have to save us all. RIP sourdough
starter August 2020 – March 2025. Coparenting
doesn't have to be terrible. It's April 1,
so let's remember we are a poet.

> I miss my dog.
> The air is attacking us.
> It is good to remember poetry.

The porch is a vortex. I am now
sick. The couch is a vortex. Flood flood
flood flood flood. I cannot teach
grown adults empathy.

Inner suffering cannot foster
outward peace.

METHOD OF LOCI

The cold Toledo Museum of Art,

> sound moving weird around sculpture,
> chandelier, and geriatric security guards
> shuffling gallery to gallery—
>
> some kind of spaceship hum. I want the bench
> in front of my favorite woman in the corner,
> my Shepard's Star, farmer with a scythe jaw
> and a sack of potatoes on her broad
> shoulder, her bare bony feet.
>
>> Her stare would help me know how to do
>> what I need to do.

A blanket on the part of Erie beach by the power plant
that has eroded away,

> as impossible to get to as the girl I was at 16
> falling in love and falling in a trap there,
> gathering sharp hornsnail shells,
>
> the polite midwestern waves rolling toward
> the sand and my sunburned ears with a warning,
>
>> but unable to reach me.

Dos Gatos coffee shop in Johnson City,

> surrounded by strangers on laptops,
> tiny cups of stern espresso and big sugary
> caramel swirl lattes being called out at the counter.
> I want to look at the new art on the walls,
>
> write a poem about a middle-aged woman
> eating a scone who falls into one of the paintings,

maybe one full of flowers and mystical-looking
trees that turn out to be dancing monsters
when you step closer,

     but happy monsters.

A pancake house far away,

     with a small yellow coffee mug sitting beside
     my plate of something covered in pecans
     and raspberries and melting butter, across from me
     a benevolent breakfast date eating eggs,
     someone who knows we're going to figure out

          each other's secrets in just a moment,
          eyes listening.

The railing of my dad's glass shop, circa 1994
on a Saturday morning in mid-September.

     I wouldn't want to be 1994 me, or even see her,
     but I'd like to watch the Ren Faire folks
     swishing and jingling toward their places
     before the gate opens in 20 minutes.
     Dad's furnace is roaring.

     A red-bearded man walks by playing his lute.
     The actors of the queen's court
     shush by in heavy velvets. I swing my bare,
     muddy, cold feet

          and wait for the bag pipes to flare.

A stiff-backed wooden chair, painted
bright teal,

beside a window with linen curtains
moving a little in the breeze from
across the fjord which carries sounds of a small
boat putting off somewhere I can't see.

The air smells of ocean and plants
that I do not know blooming around
this little cabin. My hands sit still
on a table with *rosemåling*
painted down its legs. I hold hot tea,

and the light moves into me, carrying
all the sharp blade edges of the mountains,
all the songs of the waterfalls

    as the world melts.

FORTUNE

After I cracked open the fortune cookie, crumbs falling in my lap, I read the little faded strip of paper, and it said *Make peace with the questions of your heart*, and I said *that's some bullshit right there*, and I crumpled the mean little paper because that's not even a fortune since it doesn't tell you anything about your future and it doesn't predict joy or calamity, and if I had my way I'd grab up the guy writing non-fortune fortunes like this one by the scruff of his collar and make him listen to all of my questions because I can't make peace with not knowing all these unknowable things, like why does that song about a little pink heart on a little brown raft floating out to sea slay me even 25 years later, and why is cold air tolerable but cold water isn't, and why do I gotta write these poems, just a bajillion poems gathering digital dust in their digital folder on my digital desktop, and why does water dripping on mossy rocks make me feel at home in a way that being in my home never does, and why did becoming a mother make me feel suddenly motherless, and why can't fortune cookies have actual fortunes in them anymore, and where is that baby in Norway buried, and where is my sister who I'm not supposed to know about, and was my brother's ghost watching when the Navy buried his ashes at sea, and where will I be when I finally cross the equator, and who will be holding my hand when I do, and where is dad now that he's so long dead, and am I starting to like spicy food because my taste buds are dying somehow as I cross into middle age, and what was that woman cooking in that Nigerian novel because it sounded delicious and dangerous, and when will it all be enough, and all the other questions I have, but the truth of it is, there is no little man typing up these fortunes because everything is done by computers these days because we humans have lost our ability to see the future.

THINGS I WANT TO WRITE A POEM ABOUT BUT DON'T HAVE THE ENERGY TO BECAUSE WE'RE SURVIVING HELL

The last penny being minted.

The image of a child with a map.

A sonnet about pins and needles in my arm
when I finally roll away from you at night.

The fluffy squirrels who startle me each morning,
making such racket in the dry oak leaves.

How much I would love to be a novelist.

All the tattoos I want to get.

How I wish I could be mad at my ex-husband
for all of it.

A daydream of kissing a shy redhead
in a grandpa cardigan after a square dance.

The green sea turtles no longer being classified
as endangered.

The Christmas Island shrew now being classified
as extinct.

My dead little dog who would climb into my hoodies
to keep warm in winter.

The metaphor of mom getting her cataracts
removed to restore sight.

Dad teaching me to slice an onion.

The apologies I need to give my children.

Why list poems and giant blocks of rambling text
seem all I can manage.

How living on high alert for decades has crystalized
something in my chest like a pulsing cancer.

I'M TRYING TO SOFTEN

how I live on this planet, use less fossil fuel, yes,
but also use less angry self-talk.

Smile up into the first blast of cold November.
Hold tight to myself in a hug under a scalding shower

until my brain catches its breath. Not always give
all of myself away just because it makes things easier

for someone else who's not as strong as me.
Take my battered polar bear zoo coffee cup to the barista

for my order, ask for oat milk. Call my mother more.
Stop planning how I could try to change my body

before every next big social event. Sprout radish
and beet seeds in Mason jars on my tiny kitchen counter.

Send a beam of light from my solar plexus to every
ambulance running with its siren screaming and every

funeral procession creeping the daylit road with headlights on.
Not buy most things that look alluring on the internet

newsfeed. Plan a pollinator garden with some high schoolers.
Drink water more. Try to find shade-grown coffee.

Talk about my experience as a woman online because
women doing that saved me. Run a less-than-groundbreaking

poem in my magazine for a writer who really needs a win.
Take those reusable bags to the store. Buy ugly veggies

before they throw them away. Stop trying to fix people
who need to learn the skills of self-governance and discipline.

Stop giving away all of everything in the deep, desperate
hope that will entice folks to give the same back to me.

Remember the shieldmaidens on the show we were watching
who said *We don't sing the songs. The songs are singing us.*

Mine eyes have seen the glory:
the turn of the screw,
the natural way to draw
the city in which I love you.

    Men of salt:
    close range
    warhogs.

THE NEUROSCIENCE OF PREDICTIVE BODY MEMORY

It was the damnedest thing.
The first time I met you,

I stood there, gathering
your name and your hand in mine,

and I ghost-smelled Bactine,
that terrible antiseptic spray

on my bike-wreck wounds,
my fell-out-of-the-tree wounds,

my misjudged-how-hot-the-electric-
stove-burner-was wounds.

Little white bottle, its green lid spritz
unleashing fire on the skin, a sizzle.

My eyes squinched.
My air gasped.

It has proven true, incidentally.
You scorched electric across

my raw places, those sliced
or blistered from contact

with the world. You burned it clean
in a pain worse than the original,

astringent and therapeutic.
Your scald has faded,

the cells stitching quiet
in the dark, a cushiony

band aid keeping everything
at bay while we wait

for the scab, the skin's
own shushing. My body doesn't

understand. My body only
remembers the searing chemistry

that burned so agonizing against
biology, eviscerated the world

down to the squealing slice,
you, a bright, sharp scour.

WIFE

after Savannah Sipple

B	I	N	G	O
ring	surname	shared entree	homemaker	Adam's rib
honest woman	nag	sacrifice	pants	dirty socks
Valentine	henpeck	FREE	orgasm	dirty dishes
anniversary	home-wrecker	joint account	sandwich	wine o'clock
Mx. Right	cuckold	Cinderella	white dress	obedience

AUBADE: A SCENE

Me: Why did you throw your Arby's cup in the driveway?

     Him: What?

Your cup. What was the benefit of throwing it on the ground instead of bringing in the house?

     We were running late, and I had two cups and was going to go run around all day for our family.

Oh. I thought you threw it down last night when we got out of the car. *Smile. Light tone*

     We were rushing and I needed to put those two cups in the holder.

Ah. I was mistaken. I thought it was last night, not 2 days ago. *Smile.*

     I had my hands full. I'm sorry if that offends you.

No. I said I misunderstood. I thought it was last night when we got home. My question is moot. I've done that too when in a rush and getting in the car. *Forced, light laugh.*

     … Did *you* pick it up?

…….

     ……….

Pointing to garbage bag I got out of the cabinet. I'm going to when I get out there.

     Did you pick it up?

… No.

     You didn't pick it up?

No.

Well, then the only sin is that *someone* walked past it twice and didn't pick it up.

CHANGE THE SUBJECT: A SCENE

*I'm trying not to vomit or shit my pants while I drive the kids to school.
He is riding shotgun.*

      Him: What did you have besides coffee?

Me: Two Oreos.

      You should've had some salmon patties.
            *He gestures to his open bowl of hot salmon patties stinking
            up the car.*

I'd prefer not to talk about food.

      Ok, we can change the subject and talk about…

………

      pizza.

………

      *A few minutes pass. I try gentle breathing as I break into
      cold sweat and more cramps. He puts his hand on my leg.*

      Do you usually eat Oreos in the morning?

I'd prefer not to talk about food.

      It's a word that's already been said!

I don't want to think about my gut. I'm trying to distract myself.

      Ok…. we can…. pretend.
      He takes his hand off my leg.

WHY DID YOU DO THAT: A SCENE

I tell of trying to order my lunch on my laptop, how the restaurant website sent me to another website which sent me to Apple Pay which sent me to set up an account on the iCloud. I tell of giving up and ordering with my phone, how when my coworker went to pick it up, the order was wrong, how she corrected them and supposedly they fixed it, but when I opened my bag, my lunch was still wrong.

Him: Why did you do that?

Me: Do what?

All of that.

All of what?

Why did you fuck around with the websites and all that?

I couldn't call the restaurant because it wasn't open yet.

How did everyone else get their orders correct?

.....

Their orders were correct, yes?

Yes. Mine looked correct on the screen when I ordered it.

I don't know why you would do all that.

TEXTBOOK: A SCENE

Him: I'm not going to counseling
again. Last time was fake.
You were faking.

Me: …..

That's not what you
were trying to do. That's
not what you felt.

…

It's dangerous for you
because any time you
disagree with something,
you'll say it's
gaslighting.

..

That's a buzzword
that doesn't
mean anything.

.

ON THE DAY: A SCENE VIA TEXT

The school called with a pre-recorded message from the principal about an 8th grader bringing a gun to our 13-year-old's school.

Me: It's scary.

    Him: ?

The gun at school.

    blue thumbs up

I NEVER KNOW

if I stop and pick you half a bag
of mulberries, my fingers purple and sticky,

will you be happy at my dark and sweet gift, or tell
me I should've done more, that my half bag could've been

full if I only would've inconvenienced the tree, its owner, myself,
if only I had tried, done differently, predicted that my gift wouldn't

be enough. There is a zero currently, and I don't know if this
will turn zero into positive one or negative one. And when

my gift turns zero into negative one, I feel stupid
for trying. I wish I had just left it alone,

happy with nothing, cradled quietly
in that safe, empty circle.

REACTIVE

The woman screaming in the parked car
in the junk store lot, punching the horn
over and over again, looks fucking insane.
She's screaming *shut up shut up shut up*
shut up with a punch to the horn on each *up*.
She looks wild. Irrational. Like a beast of pure
madness, making the car rock and squall
in sync with her punches, red and twisted
face slicked with snot and tears.

The man slamming the car door and stomping
across the asphalt, away from this
screaming, punching beast, raising his arms
above his head, taking a long deep breath—
he looks human, looks rational, looks loving,
adult, mature, like someone trying to encourage
calm and peace. Someone in the right.

If you look at her when she stops punching
the horn, when she grabs the steering wheel
with both hands and slams herself back
and forth in the seat as she shrieks wordlessly,
roaring until she collapses forward
into weak sobs and low moans—
she looks like her tantrum is done.

When the man eventually returns to the car,
gets in and clicks his seat belt and she drives
them home, her face a zombie glaze and his
turned out the window, it looks like he is patient
and caring and that she is returning to sanity,
that a hurricane passed and left a human
in the little car's driver's seat.

The thing is, while a house burns, flames licking
out the windows like eyelashes and billows
of smoke puffing like morning bedhead,
the blazing house looks like a furious woman,
heat blasting from her front door mouth
curling and charring the yard flowers,
threatening the whole neighborhood
with her uncontrollable rage. The man
standing at the dark edge of the street,
gas can behind his back, looks like a curious
and concerned neighbor, like maybe he
was the person to call 911, the person—
nay, *hero*— who tells everyone
this house is burning herself down.

I WALK TO THE GREAT LAKE AS THE SUN ROSE
AFTER I ADMITTED I WANTED A DIVORCE

Admitted it out loud to a lawyer friend
and a love friend, and I walk the quiet

suburban neighborhood to a nook at the end
of a road that vaguely points east.

Everything is groggy. And I look for a poem
to write with a half-assed kind of mind,

listening to some water bird in the cattails
and the freeway groaning back and forth across

the Michigan border. An early morning
boat chugs across the bay as the world pinks.

I start to speak this poem into my phone app,
July rousing itself from cool sleep, the boat heading

toward Canada, the cars crossing borders, my heart
also at a terrible threshold. Two bald eagles

drop and flap down from the cottonwood beside me
and head out to find some kind of breakfast.

ONE MONTH

It's exactly four weeks
since I handed him
the letter, said I didn't
want to be married
anymore and fled
to page one of a next
chapter. He is stung
by yellow jackets
eight times this morning
on the neck and face.
I go to the gyno
to schedule a tubal ligation,
go to the thrift store
to look for a spatula,
potato masher, and cake pan
still OK enough to use.

OUR COURT DATE

You try to get me to leave the courtroom and wait in the hallway, stress I don't need to be there since you were the one to file after I left, say you waited out in the hall when you were divorcing the first time. You say the judge and lawyer might try to trick me into saying something that would complicate and drag out the proceedings. I say I'm not going to say anything to complicate things, that the judge and lawyer are not conspiring against us, there is no reason they would be. We watch a few cases be called forth and resolved. You lean and whisper a second time that I don't need to go stand with you at the bench when our case is called, that it's better if you just handle it. I say again I'll come up with you. When your lawyer comes by, you whisper-ask him if I need to go up to the bench with you. *She's a grown woman*, he says. *She doesn't have to, but has the right to if she wants.* I am 44 and you are 55 and your lawyer just had to tell you that I am an autonomous adult. And I am suddenly transported outside our history. I suddenly see how scared you are of me. We don't fight to control things we're not afraid of. I wanted to stand like peers before this judge to unmarry like we stood before a judge 22 years before to join. But I give you this final gift you don't deserve, and I sit on the wooden pew while you stand with your lawyer and your fear before the judge and you divorce me. I am so sad for you. I am so sad for me. I am so sad for our daughters. We hug outside Subway and you wait until I break the embrace. I go to the bank to try for a loan to consolidate the financial ruin you have put me in. I'm denied because of all the late payments. I drive to a 19-year-old tattoo artist and ask her to ink a water band around my forearm, the Red Bird River where we met, Maumee Bay where we fell in love, the Ottawa River where we made one child, Cumberland Falls where we made another, the Middle Fork River where we raised them and beans and turkeys and where I gnarled and your edges serrated, Troublesome Creek that tried to kill everyone and shook me awake, Lake Erie where I paced the beach and whispered to her small waves that I was going to leave when I went home, back across the Maumee, the Ohio, and the Kentucky. That young tattoo artist is the age I was when you proposed at a truck stop in Alabama by saying *What do you think about being married to someone who is emotionally damaged?* and at the time I thought you meant you but maybe you meant me. It was definitely both of us.

Why else would we have been there, me 19 and you 30? And I take that new water inked under my skin home to my new world on the oak hill, sit quietly on my new-to-me rented couch, and feel the currents pulling me in every direction, my neck suddenly sprouting gills.

(RE)FOREST

I took an ax to my idea of what my life should be
and accepted what it was. After it dried, I split
that brittle pulp and now put it to the flames.
I hover near the heat of past dreams,
warm my hands, then nap quietly,
alone. Those newly divorced
from the future they burned
sleep heavily, solid, deep,
away from all their
remorse, guilt
and anger.

In that dream-space of brittle winter,
in 4:00 slanting light, pre-solstice,
I breathe with the mountains, their
core older than the evolution of bones.

And I ask the cold
stones exactly what
will sprout from the space
I just clearcut. Me again? Or
an overrun of eager invasives?
A hunting road? A Dollar General? What
will be here after? The microcosm of human
vision is shorter than this old hickory's, which is
shorter than the withering mountain's, which is shorter
still than that of the arcing stars which will return tonight
to the new-moon-sky dark while we gather to ask ourselves

again and again what we can possibly do.

DIVORCEE

after Savannah Sipple

B	I	N	G	O
selfish	liar	freeloader	new curtains	callous
letter	blamed	freedom	new address	bad mom
run run run	escape artist	FREE	new hope	un-lonely
tofu	floral tea	divide	new love?	brave
bitch	unfolding	poor	so poor	shhhh

LOVE IN A DEAD LANGUAGE: A BOOK SPINE POEM

Red scarf girl
in the heart of the sea,
why do they act that way?

    Not just the levees broke.

    After the funeral
    I will fight no more forever.

LITMUS

She said you can tell a lot about a person
in how they interpret a word—*a strap*—
Is this a gun? A sex toy? A tongue of leather
to beat a child with? A polyester belt to tie
a bundle of camping gear to the trailer?

She said you can tell a lot about a person
in how they talk to a slumped figure
at a bus stop, a thin dog in the snow,
a squalling child, a purple-haired barista.

She said you can tell a lot about a person
by what they want done with their corpse
when they die, what they feel insulted by,
what they do with their shoes when they step
into someone else's house, how they spend
their money and other people's money.

She said you can tell a lot about a person
by how they look at graffiti, how they look at
the weeks-long gray sky, how their breathing
changes when they hear a banjo or hissing
cat or firetruck, what happens to their face
when someone carries them a plate of food.

She said you can tell a lot about a person
by how they move or don't move through
the world, and how the world moves
or doesn't move through them.

AUTOBIOGRAPHY IN THREE SENTENCES

A creature of water, I am
offspring of a dragon
and a set of numbers.
I have tried to live on land,
this long adjustment
to solidity. Two far-off
red giant stars were born
unto me, and I crane
my neck to track their arc
and glitter across cosmos
while the day flays
myself from me.

A STORY ON MOTHER'S DAY
reading The Museum of Cheats by Sylvia Townsend Warner

Before everyone stirs, I make coffee and burrow into the couch, feeling all Instagram and BookTok-like, the luxury of a quiet moment as self-care kind of thing ya know? I open the short story collection I'm working my way through, written by a lesbian in WWII England, 1947. I open to "Step This Way," a story about a girl and her mother who are in another woman's house, and they are seeking an abortion for the girl. They discuss rations, the girl's mean, unemployed father. There is no mention of the baby's father. The mother is pushing the girl, and in the end, is the one most afraid when the woman calls the girl back. And the girl goes alone. I think of "Hills Like White Elephants," how that woman was pushed by her man, how the procedure is described as *letting the air in*, that it was never more specific, that *abortion* is deduced by readers. It is the same with this story. And I think of me at 16 on a Saturday, beginning to miscarry three days before my scheduled abortion. How I went in for the emergency D&C by myself, leaving my mother in the waiting room. How the father was not there. How for millennia, women have had so little control over our bodies, how we are the reason humanity exists, how pregnancy and childbirth is the deadliest endeavor modern folks do, and most women do it multiple times. The second story I read, "Daphnis and Chloe," is about a solider on leave who wants to go out dancing, but his girl is afraid of the bombings and she won't go out. I think of COVID killing my kids' aunt and stealing years' worth of their childhood. I think of their active shooter drills at school and the 7-year-old saying *Corbin looked out the window mom, and he could've been shot!* I think of when I said I was going to a Pride festival and the 10-year-old said *But mom, those are the places that get bombed!* And motherhood is too much on this Mother's Day, truthfully, too much on most days. I close the WWII book here at the potential dawning of WWIII, or at least another Civil War. I don't know what to do besides warm this cold coffee.

ORBIT

disco_fort
m_nsoon
_error
eart_ling
p_rpetual
ac_obat
galact_c
u_done
_ravity

DAUGHTER VILLANELLE

It's an old story, being a daughter,
the dirt molecules and galaxy dust a brood
always under the threat of water.

Women roiling fore and aft, fraught
rules about bodies, movement, and food
telling stories of how to be a daughter.

Rice falls from fists to promise-scatter
across kitchen or wedding parking lot mud—
anywhere with threat of water,

I want to believe it's not bridle and halter,
the way we slipstitch and knot this love
into the cold stories of being daughters.

Night storms slam and we shutter
under covers, lonely and hopefully a good
ways away from the threat of water.

The red cast of our postures matter,
the shadow, scab, bruise, and blood
across the old story of being a daughter
always tangled in threads of water.

TAKING THE TEENAGERS TO THE TRAMPOLINE PARK

A trip out for one of their birthdays, they don
neon socks and run full tilt
away from the front desk.
Within moments, kids leap and bounce,
long yellow hair a flapping cape,
copper a frizzling halo,
curly brown a streaking arc.
Strobe lights and shifting walls of colors,
thumping electronic music and radio hits
accompany their unlanguaged communication.
Friends on a balance beam knock
each other off to be swallowed
by a pit of foam blocks.
Voices becoming hoarse with screaming,
shrieking, laughing. Leg muscles
and lungs burning from running, dropping,
rolling, a game of tag in a flying, leaping dash
across surfaces of varying reality—
solid, solid-ish, springing—comical cartoon physics
as they bounce off walls and launch
themselves toward the ground.
Like clumsy hummingbirds
they momentarily alight by my bench,
red-faced and humid, vibrant
and cracked open, to chug water and pant
then dart off again. I carry empty
water bottles to the recycle bin
and tap at my sternum.
They will sing songs DJed from a phone
the entire hour drive home, all caterwauling
in flat falsettos, razzing each other
between verses, hip to hip
in the dark back seat.

I am happy for them.
This was my goal.
Teenhood, with friends, unmolested,
unassaulted, unpregnant, untraumatized,
unsold, unbent, unaddicted, awash in choices,
an ability to say no, bodies their own,
unruptured, unabraded, 13 and 16
and still actual children, their own ideas
of who they are and what their bodies
are for. They fly through this cold
warehouse air, streaked red, purple,
pink, orange, ungrounded
in the good way, gasping in the good
way, blood racing in the good way,
physics pliable, bodies and futures
undetermined, and I am burning
in my heart watching them,
heads whipped, arms flailing,
gravity pulling so predictably
but the whole room an accomplice
to defy it even for just 2 seconds at a time,
again and again, making that pull down
into a soft, bouncy landing, not a crash,
a cushion of foam turned into a squealing battle,
blue and green blocks hurled with a soft,
flopping collision. No thud, no split,
no blood. Pretend danger and all around
a reciprocating give which cradles them,
absorbs their weight and momentum
and redirects it, flinging them back,
laughing into the air. Everything taking
the energy of their bodies and giving it back
to them in full, uncorrupted, unsickened.

I am burning in my heart, watching
their safety.
Their flight.

I am burning in my heart
thinking of all I did not have
and all I did.
I am burning 2 chambers in fizzy joy,
2 chambers in sour sadness,
old grief for a child who did not know
what it could've been like.
To leap like that.
To breathe in a body like that.
To have faith and safety like that
in a world designed to cushion me,
in a world designed specifically for my delight.
To be manipulating the rules of the world
unalone and uncauterized.
For the border between the world
and me to be like this.
I am 42 and 16 and 13 and 8,
watching these laughing bodies
hold hands and leap
without risk or injury.

My heart is burning
as I watch them fly.

WHERE TO FIND MY BODY IN MY HOMETOWN WHEN I DIE

Though it is the highest land feature in town, I am not
in the city dump. 30 years of my garbage is there
but that can't be of much interest to the likes of you.
However, if you are driving toward the dump, do
you see the railroad tracks behind the industrial park?
Follow those tracks on foot for the length of time
it takes you to recite all the cities you've slept in
as an adult. When finished, stop, look under
the brushy tangle beside you. You'll find my pelvis bone
in the shadow. Beware, there may be a family of mice
in the hollow nook my children passed through.

At Rudy's Hot Dog restaurant, you know the one
near the marina, you'll need to go inside.
Walk to the back, and on the greasy orange-topped
booth in the corner, you'll find my hands, folded neatly
as in prayer. Hidden beneath their bony tent,
you'll find my liver. Get yourself a strawberry malt
and grilled cheese to go before you leave.

Between the golf course and the projects, you'll find
Manhattan Marsh Nature Preserve, a soupy, boardwalked
descendant of the Great Black Swamp. Follow the trail
until you find a tree with a bald eagle's nest high in the canopy.
You're gonna have to climb up there. You're gonna
have to want it. Up there, in the heavy nest,
are my breasts, unincubated, useless, and pale.

In late spring, when the Lake Erie mayfly hatch shows
on the Doppler radar, prep yourself a picnic basket
and borrow your buddy's pontoon. Go out on the bay, out
to the islands. Not any of those with names on maps
or with discernible human presence. Find one
that is a little dollop in the middle of the lake and drop

anchor and trudge ashore. Have your picnic.
As the mayfly swarm approaches, pay attention
to the females. They live about 5 minutes after the larval stage.
The males get a whole 2 days. Stand up once the first one
lands on you. Dig. About a foot down in the sand,
you'll find my feet. One will have a gash on the sole
from stepping on underwater broken glass when I was 8.
There is no explanation why it would still be bleeding
all these decades later like Lake Erie stigmata.

Step into my momma's house, the one she's been in
since 1964, and don't worry about a key—it's never locked—
and don't worry about knocking—you don't wanna wake her
from her nap in the blue corner chair. Right there
is an out-of-tune piano. If you open the bench seat lid,
there are my lungs, wrapped in sheet music—one
in *Jesu, Joy of Men's Desiring* and the other
in *Jesus Christ Superstar*. Don't let the cat out as you leave.
If momma wakes up, make her a cup of hot tea
and a peanut butter and mayonnaise sandwich.

My rattly rope of spine is hanging from a clothesline
in the backyard of an old Hungarian lady on the east side.
She is blind and doesn't know it's there. She heard
the sound like a dull pottery windchime and she thinks
it's coming from her neighbor's across the fence.
The boy who mows the yard can't hear it over
his headphones and the mower, and he never
looks up from the striping green to see it.

At the Meijer parking lot by the last I-75 exit,
there are a dozen Tesla charging stations in a row.
In this blue-collar Jeep-building town, they are always
empty except when some academic from Ann Arbor

is swinging through on their way to Columbus.
You will find a thin braid of my copper brown hair,
streaked gray, tied around each charging cable.

My skull was used as a Halloween porch decoration,
then sold at a garage sale for $15, and now is on
a teenage boy's shelf, wearing sunglasses, an unlit
Marlboro between my teeth which have been painted
in a variety of sparkly nail polishes. The boy
does not know this is a real skull. Leave it for him.
He sometimes talks to it, and he needs someone to talk to.
He's going through a lot these days.

At the art museum, there is a painting of a gorgeous
woman. She has a sickle tied to her belt and is carrying
a load from the field above her head. It's a dusky twilight.
She is barefoot and looks at you like she knows you
want to kiss her. She is not interested. Pay attention
to the shuffling security guards as they rotate between rooms.
When you're alone with her, lift her frame. In an envelope
taped to the wall, you'll find my ears, listening and deaf.

My lips and heart were lost long ago. You will not find
them. Not in this town anyway. However, you can find a linen
pouch holding my wrist and ankle bones tucked behind
a book of poetry with the word *ratio* in the title on a shelf
in the university library, and if you take the pouch out under
a new moon in autumn, shake it while reading
your favorite poem from that book, and clatter
those fragile bones onto the ground, you might
figure out where the lips and heart are. Here's a clue
to help: if you travel south, time moves forward
or backward depending upon the season.

In a tangle of driftwood, cigarette butts, and soda
bottles by the dyke at the end of one of the streets, rocking
gently in the Ottawa River slurry, are my femurs, radii,
ulnas, tibias, humeri, and fibulas. My intestines, kidneys,
and uterus were in this tangle, but the fish and birds
like such soft tissue. They are long gone.

My sluggish mush of brain was buried in a school yard
under a mulberry, but something dug it up, drug it out
to the street. When startled by a passing car, the scavenger
abandoned it in the middle of the asphalt. It was squished
and squelched into a smear that was washed into
the sewer by the next day's rainstorm.

Our parakeets flew off when we were little. Their cage
was on the porch and a storm blew up and the bottom
dropped off and they were gone. Brother and I walked
the neighborhood, in futile effort and big sadness,
looking in the trees for their little puff of butter cream yellow
and Arabian sea blue. We didn't find them of course.
Nobody expected us to. I don't know what we thought
we'd do if we *did* find them. You must now wander
the neighborhoods like that, looking up at the trees.
My ribs have flown off like those doomed birds, sternum a hinge
and rib bones making two skeletal wings. They are trembling
in a tree. This the first time they've flown more than
across a living room, finally free of the cage of my body,
trembling in a tree as darkness approaches
and children wander around crying.

What about the eyes, you say. Honey, those
are in your pocket already. You stole them from me
before I was even dead.

MAPS WE FORGET TO BRING: A BOOK SPINE POEM

Eyes glowing at the edge of the woods,
something's rising—
     perfect black
     appetite,

          the girl singer
          driving with the dead.

BEING POLITICALLY NEUTRAL DURING FASCIST AMERICA

Someone sets another person on fire.

You don't intervene because
you don't want to offend

the people cheering on the flames.

REASON 1: NOVEL READING

> Experiences documented to exacerbate illness
> and lead to admission to West Virginia Hospital
> for the Insane 1864-1889

If, hypothetically, a woman would read,
let's say 100 books a year,
in what ways could that make fertile ground
for mental illness to take root and bloom?
> To see the world as it was, is,
> should've been, could be, can't be,
> has never been, will be for someone
> but not for her…

To take into her synapses a thousand or more lives
each decade. To have those voices whispering
to her in an untraceable way so we can't tell
> where one wave ends
> and another wave begins
> and where the waves themselves
> end so that the ocean can begin.

To hallucinate whole worlds, splicing
herself between existences, real and read
> back and forth a dozen times each hour
> with each interruption from her dog,
> chatty husband, sore neck,
> car honking out in the street.

Those landscapes, spacescapes, mindscapes,
facts, confessions, thwarted lives,
> all that seeing behind the curtain
> to what they themselves don't know about themselves,
> all those nightmares and love affairs
> shared with phantoms.

A blue whale,
a child locked in a tower,
a train trestle spanning a ravine,
jumbled with the other realities
of varying realness,
temporary escape that deposits her
back where she is, listening to voices

encoded in abstract black shapes on a page,
all held in the fragile bowl of her skull.

REASON 2: UTERUS

> Experiences documented to exacerbate illness
> and lead to admission to West Virginia Hospital
> for the Insane 1864-1889

Imaginary female trouble

What's that line about if we judged
a fish by its ability to climb a tree?
If women never speak or sing or write,
all those words never exist. How pathological
words would be when their smoke slips
out between the door and doorjamb.

Hysteria

Hysterectomy—Hysteria. Insanity
from the uterus. A fish can't climb a tree.
What wild beast bleeds for 7 days
without dying? What wild sorcery
in the belly's cauldron to summon
a whole living child from two specks
we can't even see with naked eyes.

Menstrual derangement

If her body's purpose is to be the cause
and receptacle of his ejaculation
and then the expulsion point of a child,
this renegade week of blood she takes for herself
disregards the purpose of her chemistry,
disregards what he gave, not making
a damn thing with it, bleeding it back out.

Suppression of menses

And what about when her purpose
isn't to make him a child from his orgasm?

Uterine derangement

Back to this? White-coated men
can't imagine being a gate between worlds,
riding the vapors, tremors, and invisible
magnetisms of holding that portal in their core.

Female disease

All these X chromosomes charging through
the world, dittoing themselves like a virus.

REASON 3: HUSBANDS

Experiences documented to exacerbate illness
and lead to admission to West Virginia Hospital
for the Insane 1864-1889

Ill treatment by husband

Desertion by husband

Domestic affliction

Domestic trouble

What was that recent study? The one that showed
women's happiness increases with their age
because they are freed from childbearing?
The one that showed they're happier
when they become widowed?
When they're single?
That divorce can
cure terror
and IBS?

HOW MANY WAYS DOES MY GOVERNMENT HATE ME

Let me count a few ways:

I was born in a body with a vagina and uterus.
I am the child of an immigrant.
I am the child of a working mother.
I have been molested and sexually assaulted by multiple white cisgender men.
I was a pregnant teenager.
I have scheduled an appointment for an abortion.
I had miscarriages, one that necessitated an emergency D&C.
I was a first-generation college student.
I earned a bachelor's degree.
I earned a master's degree.
I earned a doctorate degree.
I have used WIC.
I have used Medicaid.
I have declared bankruptcy.
I used student loans.
I have paid back 176% of what I borrowed, and it has only taken 12% off my principle.
I am an educator.
I am a reader.
I am a writer.
I have been on unemployment.
I vote.
I have Narcan in my car.
I love the people with disabilities in my family.
I love the queer and trans people in my family.
I love the black and indigenous people in my family.
I love the non-American people in my family.
I watched poor people steal from Kroger's and did not stop them.
I birthed female children.
I teach those children all sorts of things.

I belong to no religion.
I have had relationships with men and women and others.
I came out as queer on inauguration day 2017 because fuck Donald Trump.
I believe in facts and logic and fairness.
I believe in the Constitution.
I believe in kindness.
I believe in consent.
I believe war is evil.
I understand what a damn pronoun is and am not scared of them.
I have fought hard for my healing.
I work with people who believe in culture, opportunity and education.
I teach queer kids their voice matters and what happened to them wasn't their fault.
I teach old women their voice matters and what happened to them wasn't their fault.
I am learning to decenter men.
I am learning to decenter whiteness.
I am learning to decenter capitalistic, hyper-individualistic dogma.
I hope daily for his swift removal from power.
I am writing this and sharing it out loud.

CORDELIA
a love letter to my trauma response

In a strip mall suite in Denver, a man, grinning
and reeking of pot, introduced himself
as Slug and I paid him to tattoo your name
on my thigh, a classic banner over a heart.

I've never met you, a fabrication really,
a self-invented therapeutic tool. See,
when my solar plexus would prickle with fear,
when my molecules began shrinking

to appease or please, when I was crashed
down by a waterfall, pinned on the cold, slick
rocks like the whole world was waterboarding me,
I used to punch my thigh, right there where your

name is now, punch it until I could breathe
again, bruises blooming with the swelling
over the next day like slow hydrangeas.
You're my trauma response, I guess,

a master thermometer, taking the temperature
of everyone's psychoses, your obedient
protocol of self-preservation calculating the math
of everyone's motivations, blueprinting the safest

way through a moment. And I thank you
for keeping me safe, my heart of a lion, my
meticulous observer. I know you keep memories
from me because I see you adjust to magnetic

fields I can't detect, respond to bells I can't hear
ringing. I trust you that I don't need to hear them
because you got my back. But we're out
of the war zone, I think. We needed a better way

to communicate. So now instead of bludgeoning
my body to turn off your lockdown alarms,
I talk to you. I know you've heard me, how
I shush you, say *We're ok, Cordelia. We're safe.*

I know you hear me because you have released
my hitching chest and let me pull in a breath
after I thank you for your diligence and gently
ask you to let my ribs go, let these lungs expand.

You have turned off the 20,000-lumen searchlight
and let the room fall back into a soft glow
when I've assured you there is no monster here.
We are learning to communicate, you and I.

The red ink of your heart scabbed and cracked,
scarred my skin like stretch marks, my only tattoo
to do that, and of course that is a poem, as is
this way we hold each other's hand, which is our own,

drag ourselves behind the waterfall to assess
what may or may not be an actual threat without
the crushing safety measures dashing us
into foam. We are soaked and cold, bruised,

disoriented, and it is still too loud to think straight,
but we will not drown in this moment. We can
plot our way out and find somewhere to hunker
down and warm up, unclench. We can maybe

dream of a garden, a yard with dogs playing.
I've got the watch now, Cordie. You can dissolve
your vigilance and let go of yourself until you float
away. I will bring your name on my skin to all future

cascades and whisper the persistent mist full
of my gratitude for your care, how I survived
because you paid attention without ceasing.
And dare I end this poem with a rainbow for us?

no libraries no museums no thinking no funding for jobs that help dyslexic kids in the mountains to read no educational placards on North Carolinian Confederate statues contextualizing the bronze man no books no information about women astronauts on websites no museum no thinking no art that demonstrates nuance no art that doesn't praise the master no brown people no black people no trans people no children who are US citizens to undocumented parents no due process no books no learning no honesty no honesty no honesty no honesty no fairness no education no equality no health care no retirement no maternity leave no gender but this box no thinking no science no facts no intersex no brown no languages no families no helping no books no environment no truth no us no consent no consent no consent no Constitution no due process no books no thinking no truth for the children no freedom of religion no freedom of speech no gun registrations no Muslims no students no truth no speaking no listening no learning no pronouns no you no me no he no she no they no us no us no us no us no us no us no we the people no unalienable rights for most no books no reading no facts no facts no balance no society no Holocaust Museum no due process no facts no give me your tired no your poor no your huddled masses no protection from enemies foreign or domestic no protection from elected enemies no books no art no truth no access no us no hope no us no home no us no whole no us no with liberty and justice for all

FROM CREEK TO COAST : A DUPLEX POEM

for my friends who survived Eastern KY flooding in July 2022
and then survived Helene in September 2024

This water is life and death:
the clouds, the blood, the hurricane.

       Swirling clouds bleed a hurricane
       into our nightmares after love,

and hours of nightmares fuse love
to lightning flash and daydream.

       Fright flashes in your daydream
       of calm, oceanside, sweet kisses.

Calmed by ocean's salt kiss,
we forget the monumental rage of flood.

       We forget the monument, how raging floods
       bomb into torn-apart, drifting homes.

We bow toward rifting homes
because water is life, and death.

Y'ALL. YOUR GOD IS PISSED

and I don't know how you don't know it.
She's standing at the back screen door

of the kitchen, thin brown hair in spongy
pink rollers, light blue fuzzy house coat tied tight

around a middle-aged belly, Pall Mall pinched
in spotted fingers, smoke curling toward the ceiling.

She is glaring at you as you slam through the door.
You thump past without a hello, without a kiss

on the cheek, without an explanation of where you've been,
why you're late. God glares over Her glasses,

sees your empty hands. She only asked you to do
one thing today, bring home tomato sauce and garlic bread

because She was going to make your favorite supper
just to be nice. You stomp into the living room,

collapse into the groaning recliner like a tower
that's been demolitioned. The TV squeals alive.

God drags on Her cigarette, blows out a cloud,
the beginnings of an apocalyptic thunderstorm.

WHAT I DON'T WANT TO ADMIT BEFORE WE DEPART

I'm scared to write all this.
I'm scared for anyone to read all this.

I lied and cheated and tore down
the world trying to feel differently.

I have owed apologies. I am owed apologies.

The propaganda story of us, I swallowed it
whole, I was so starved.

Honesty is a murky glossary.

I need a good therapist. Probably medication.
Perhaps some gentle religion and a stern lover.

I passed on some generational curses
I should have pruned.

The sun making the dried oranges I hung
in the window of my new place glow
each evening is the closest I have
ever been to knowing god.

TOMORROW WILL BE DIFFERENT: A BOOK SPINE POEM

The glass castle:

a room of one's own,
three cups of tea,
        the girl from the sea,
        six thousand years of bread.

FINDING A NEW WAY TO PRAY
at Pennyrile State Resort Park

Start in a September gazebo folding the night's dark thoughts
into dark shapes on the new page of morning. Move to a moth

with 16 wing eyes watching from a car hood, patiently
enduring the inconvenience of your gasp and camera.

Find he's a hackberry emperor butterfly and at 45 you don't know
the technical difference – moth / butterfly. Red leaves against

teal water, tree root stepping stones. Fog. Fog always as prayer—
cloying and damp, quick to burn off but also to return.

Be thankful for gravity, for DNA and Spirit calling beside you,
calling attention to a slow woodpecker, to a scritching squirrel.

Prayer as a sudden and unexpected crumbled house in the trees,
beams dissolving under moss, and the stubborn stone chimney,

the throat through which woodsong sang for generations.
Oaks buttressing the stained-glass windows of September,

boulder gargoyles tumbled down from Pangean mountain heights.
Look at the ferns at the foot of your child beside this history.

Look when they point at a pile of deer skat in the clover.
Consider again what you want done with your body when you die—

consider how cycling to become deer skat in clover would be
an honorable end to your story when you give up your ghost.

Send a smiling photo to your tender-voiced lover. Scoop a title
for a new poem from the lake shimmer. Prayer as feeling

the morning rising like incense smoke to sting your eyes and snag
your breath a little and trail through all the moments ticking forward

to the next bell tolling us back to worship. Prayer as being alive
and paying deliberate, unceasing attention to it as if it were holy.

GOOD LORD WILLING &

the creek is rising today—
        muddy brown roar,
                branches,
                basketballs,
                Mt. Dew bottles of tobacco spit
                        riding the churning current past.
The power is out and torrents
        blast down mountainsides
                & leap off cliff edges & road cuts.
        Ditches are glutted,
                tadpoles swept down toward the confluence,
                the corn planted yesterday
                a loss.
Plastic Walmart bags snag in the river weeds
        like ghost decoration in mid-November,
                out of place and out of time.
                        The sky cracks open again,
        our bridge is already underwater,
                us stranded all weekend.
That's ok. We got nowhere to go.
                Everything will be scoured fresh tomorrow,
                the metallic flood smell
                        mixing with thick lilac & sugary katsura.

I've been gone two and a half years.
                I don't wish you were here, but I'd like you to see
                        this flood.

PERIMENOPAUSE HAIBUN

Congratulations! The 30 years of your internal chemistry being in a flux every single day and how you bled for the sake of the species while sitting in 6th grade math class and while grocery shopping and talking to your boss and burying your dead dog and all that, will now be rewarded with itchy ear canals, trouble swallowing, heart palpitations, your period being two weeks late or early to derail that scheduled romantic weekend, bloating, night sweats, brain fog, anxiety, depression, muscle aches, inflammation, unexpected full-on hemorrhaging while on a 6-mile hike in the woods with strangers, weight gain, thinning hair, vaginal dryness, hot flashes, migraines, increased weepiness, joint pain, forgetfulness, going from having a good day to wanting to burn the world in the time that it takes to fit a pack of D batteries in the already-full family junk drawer, sudden food sensitivities, new allergies, decreased libido, UTIs, stress incontinence, dry skin, constipation, brittle nails, irritability, breast soreness, dizziness, fatigue, insomnia, tingling extremities, heartburn, trouble finding words, panic attacks, burning mouth, difficulty concentrating, tinnitus, dry eyes, low confidence and self-worth, misogynistic jokes, and more!

> Womanhood explained:
> Even the cessation of
> bleeding will hurt us.

LOTTERY

The tongue says that your name, written
on this paper is some kind of proof.

> The wise hand wipes the sleep from eyes
> and greets the sound of the neighbor's rooster.

The tongue says please burn me to ashes,
I want to fluff away into gray silence.

> The wise hand opens the appendices,
> tries to find the sounds of yellow in October.

The tongue says come here, stay the night.

> The wise hand turns the car key, engine
> turning over in a dark parking lot.

The tongue says I am so hungry, make me forget myself.

> The wise hand twists the blinds closed.

UPON DRIVING AWAY FROM YOUR HOMETOWN

This sadness is a shark,
      ancient and without bone,
      cartilage allowing it to squeeze
      into small spaces.
This sadness is a shark.
      It has to keep moving to stay
      alive. It never sleeps.
This sadness is a shark.
      Year after year, it sprouts
      extra rows of teeth.

This sadness is a blackberry thicket.
      It grows unpampered
      and is near impossible to eradicate
      once it has set root.
This sadness is a blackberry thicket,
      a random burst of spike
      and thorn, little dark jewels
      hidden in underbrush.
This sadness is a blackberry thicket,
      always tart enough to draw
      your mouth, made palatable
      by deliberate silver-lining sweetening.

This sadness is a zoo,
      expensive and gaudy, leaving
      feet aching and shoulders sunburned.
This sadness is a zoo,
      the wild recreated in pretend
      containable habitats. Even the animals
      can tell the difference.
This sadness is a zoo,
      open 9-5 today, free parking

with your membership. Stand outside
the glass and gape. Point your finger
when you spot a living body.

COLOR PALETTE FOR NEXT SEASON

I need you to hold me in gold,
that augmentable fantasy,
that metallic spotlight.

Hold me in fuchsia, the slightly
bittersweet chorus that comes
around again and again.

Hold me in heavy brown, heavy
as the pause before a door
closes one last time.

Hold me in gray that knows itself
so well it's black.

WITHOUT A PARACHUTE

You return to the page to see
your own face in the ink
and what hunger is, however
salty they both may be.

The glow in this room
is deceptive. It's not coming
from the sun. It's coming
from my dwarf star heart.

You return to me to again
measure my wingspan
against the wall. I can now
reach as wide as a turkey vulture.

We should not tell anyone
how to respond to their own
oppression. You return to the sink
to wash your hands of it.

DISUNION REFUTATION

I love you, America, by which I mean I love you in the Statue of
Liberty and her huddled masses kind of way, in the first brick thrown
at Stonewall way, in the Affrilachian poets way, the Underground
Railroad, the underground punk show, the backyard cookout way, in
the students walking out in protest of ICE way, in the mutual aid way,
the little free library way. I love you in the fuck Columbus Day way,
the fuck Donald Trump way, the there never were good old days way,
in the no one is illegal on stolen land built by stolen hands kind of
way. I love you in the Pride month way, the Women's History Museum
way, the Rock & Roll Hall of Fame way, the taco truck kind of way,
the Roe v. Wade way, the Brown v. Board of Education way, the First
Amendment way. America, I love you in the cornbread in a skillet way,
the trans folks receiving gender-affirming care just like cis folks do way,
the AAPI month reading list way, ACLU way, the NAACP way, the
ADA way. I love you in the community college way, the National Parks
way, the I have a dream way, the cheesy grits way, the mutt running
through a muddy creek way, the Appalachians are older than the rings
of Saturn way, the No Kings marches way. I love you in a circle of
little girls in jingle dresses at the powwow way. In the Black women
mathematicians being celebrated for getting us to the moon way. I love
you in the trick-or-treating way, the Nancy Drew way, and bra burning
way, the Humane Society way, the US Postal Service way. I love you in
the Girl Scouts defending a transgirl's belonging in a troop way. The
strawberry milkshake and fried pickles way. The Make-A-Wish way.
The Appalshop way. I love you in the delta blues and bluegrass way, the
red necks at Blair Mountain way, the middle school science fair way, the
bag pipes drowning out a hateful campus preacher way. I love you in the
Pell Grant way, the sit-in way, the PBS and state fair way. The Medicare
and Medicaid way. The Sesame Street and Reading Rainbow way.
The Islamic mosque rising out of the cornfields just south of Toledo,
Ohio way. I love you the Maria Tallchief way, the Ani Difranco and
Dolly Parton way, the Mr. Rogers and Bob Ross and Utah Phillips way.
The polio vaccine way, the NASA way, the bison being reintroduced
into Yellowstone way, the Narcan and harm reduction way, the boo
at hideous cybertrucks way. I love you in an hour of watching videos
of Latino families erupting with joy during the Super Bowl halftime

show way. The Clean Water Act and Clean Air Act way. The Loving v. Virginia, the Obergefell v. Hodges, the Lilly Ledbetter Fair Pay Act way. I love you in the pronouns in your email signature way. I love you in the Kentucky agate way. Dammit America, I love your public libraries so so hard. Your community gardens and old men sitting on Midwest porches together. I love your Great Lakes. Your Chihuahua desert. Your 3,000-year-old trees. Your brand-new spewing lava. Your glaciers and Everglades. Your July fireworks exploding above the baseball field while my children gasp up at the night, their faces thrown suddenly into color. I love you in the way we have to, sternly and without coddling—there is so much dangerous about you now (always has been). You have pus rising up from the depths of deep, vile infection. I love you enough to help lance the wound and scour us clean.

ALL I KNOW OF THE SOUL IS A SEA WAVE

I sit adrift on this porch as if on a raft at sea,
as if the acorns at my feet were collected shells,

as if that brash crow was a brash ring-billed gull, as if
the sound of the road trailing the bottom of this hill

was wave crashes, as if the November morning chill
on my skin was sunburn, as if the overcast, faded sky

and its impending rain were sunglare making me squint.
I sit, adrift and asking this ocean swell mountain

to grant me wisdom, like billions before me, stepping out
into our origin to decipher the future. I think of an old Zen poem—

something like *we sit together, the mountain and me,*
until only the mountain remains. And if that isn't all the wisdom

we need, like Hallmark stitched it on a pillow or AI pasted it
in curly font on an image of an orange sunset. It all matters,

and none does, because even the mountain eventually
will no longer be here. Do what you feel is right during this brief

sea wave of your life because soon enough it will, you will,
be drawn back into the salt of the divine and disappear.

SPOTIFY PLAYLIST FOUND POEM

By and by, tomorrow
the vagabond will make
silver linings of these
rivers and roads.
Dearly departed, I'm with you
and all the debts I owe.
Believe, wildfire changes
the otter heart. Call it dreaming
at the ends of the earth.
It's all we ever knew.

TWO OR THREE THINGS I KNOW FOR SURE:
A BOOK SPINE POEM

Don't look behind you—
the sun does shine.

On earth, we're briefly gorgeous
illusions
from seed to bloom.

> When women were birds,
> walking where we lived
> in the house of wilderness,
> I was here.

ACKNOWLEDGMENTS

Thank you, always, to my Appalachian writing community, my creative soulmates and biggest supporters. I am grateful for the gatherings where many of these poems were born or refined including the Appalachian Writers' Workshop, the Mountain Heritage Literary Festival, the Mildred Haun Conference, and assorted classes, workshops, gatherings, and retreats. Special thanks to all those participating in the Hindman Settlement School's cohort of the Stafford Challenge. Many of these poems began during our time together.

Thank you specifically to Marianne Worthington for guidance on this manuscript and much else. You were my first teacher at Hindman and the first person to publish me in the Appalachian community. You are a beacon and a buoy. Thank you to Kari Gunter-Seymour for letting me sit in on your Makery class marking the 250th year of the United States, which sparked several of these poems. Thank you for the work you do celebrating Appalachian women and for including me in it. Thank you especially to Katerina Stoykova for seeing value in this manuscript and for helping me midwife it into the world. Thank you for helping me feel brave when I needed it most.

Thank you to the women on TikTok and other online platforms who taught me about narcissistic personality disorder, CPTSD, divorce, perimenopause, trauma and healing. Thank you to friends Rebecka Fugate, Amy Le Ann Richardson, and Mandi Fugate Sheffel for helping keep me upright during the tumultuous past few years. Thank you to Maryann Zoll, for being the first person to offer me guidance through divorce.

Thank you to Tyler Barrett. You have been an unexpected pivot in my life. Thank you for holding my hand while I shook myself awake. Thank you for loving me and for teaching me many beautiful new things. I am grateful that terrible flood made our worlds intersect.

Big love to my momma, the queen, Judith Jorgenrud. Thank you for life and for showing me the value of education and self-sufficiency. Big love to my sister, Jill Lawrence. Thank you for showing me how to be a survivor and how to speak the truth, especially when it's difficult. Big love to my brother, Brian Parker. Thank you for the epic soundtrack during our weird childhood and for caring for the homeplace.

Always, the biggest love to my children, Kelsey Pearl and Violet. You are the best thing I've ever done and ever will, and I love you bigger than the sky. You are such wonderful humans.

Thank you to the publications where some of these poems were previously featured:

"From Creek to Coast: A Duplex Poem": *Had I a Dove*, 2025

"Good Lord Willing &": *Women of Appalachia Project Women Speak vol 8*, 2022

"(Re)Forest": *The Stafford Challenge 2024-2025*, 2025

"Upon Driving Away from Your Hometown": *Southern Poetry Anthology: vol 3 Contemporary Appalachia*, 2025

"Y'all. Your God is Pissed": *Women of Appalachia Project Women Speak vol 11*, 2025

NOTES

"First 100 Sentences": the quote "Life is like sea foam. Give yourself away like the sea" is from the movie *Y Tu Mamá También*.

"I'm Trying to Soften": the quote "We don't sing the songs. The songs are singing us" is from the show *Beforeigners*.

"All I Know of the Soul is a Sea Wave": the passage is from "Zazen on Ching-t'ing Mountain" by Li Bai, translated by Sam Hamill.

"Fortune": the song about the little pink heart is "Grey" by Ani Difranco.

ABOUT THE AUTHOR

Melissa Jørgenrud Helton is Literary Arts Director of Hindman Settlement School, a cultural nonprofit in Knott County, Kentucky. Her work has been published in *Shenandoah*, *Women Speak*, *Still: The Journal*, *Anthology of Appalachian Writers*, *Norwegian Writers Climate Campaign*, and more. Her chapbooks include *Inertia: A Study* (Finishing Line Press), and *Hewn* (Workhorse), and her first full length collection is *A Middle-Aged Woman Rages* (Accents Publishing). She is editor of the anthology *Troublesome Rising: A Thousand-Year Flood in Eastern Kentucky* (University Press of KY) and *Untelling*, the literary and arts magazine of Hindman Settlement School. Her work has been supported through the Kentucky Foundation for Women, and has been awarded the George Scarbrough Poetry Prize, the Emma Bell Miles Nonfiction Prize, has been nominated for Best of the Net, and once won her a piece of key lime pie. She has been honored with the Mildred Haun Award of Excellence and designation as a Kentucky Colonel, and she is a dual citizen in the United Kingdom.

www.ingramcontent.com/pod-product-compliance
Lightning Source LLC
Chambersburg PA
CBHW022110050726
47591CB00002B/745